WATER

WATER
A View from Japan

text by
Bernard Barber

photographs by
Dana Levy

New York • WEATHERHILL • Tokyo

水 The character for water is pronounced *mizu* or *sui* in Japanese, depending on whether one uses the native Japanese word (*mizu*) or the Japanese version of the Chinese pronunciation (*sui*). Combined with another character—and there are literally hundreds of such combinations—水 forms words and phrases whose meanings are associated with water. They range from expected ones such as *suiryoku* (water power), *mizutama* (drop of water), and *mizuta* (paddy field) to others such as *mizu shōbai* (the entertainment business), *mizukakeron* (a futile argument), and *suibaku* (hydrogen bomb).

The calligraphy shown opposite is from an eighteenth-century copybook. Because it is written with four strokes basic to brush calligraphy, the character for water is one of those always used for practice.

First Edition, 1974

Published by John Weatherhill, Inc., 149 Madison Avenue, New York, N.Y. 10016, with editorial offices at 7–6–13 Roppongi, Minato-ku, Tokyo 106, Japan. Protected by copyright under terms of the International Copyright Union; all rights reserved. Printed and first published in Japan.

LCC 74–76103   ISBN 0–8348–0097–7

CONTENTS

PREFACE

In Japan water is everywhere. It seems that behind every pine tree there is a bay or river or lake. It is a part of almost every aspect of life—a part of religion, of art, of work, of relaxation. It is a means of support, a cause of destruction. It is a part of birth and a part of death.

It is not surprising that the three views of Japan most famous and most sought out by Japanese tourists are all water views: Matsushima Bay with its pine-clad islands; Miyajima with its shrine buildings stretching out across the water to the giant *torii* (sacred gate) which rises from the sea; and Ama no Hashidate (the Bridge of Heaven), a thin, sandy spit of land which ties together the two sides of Miyazu Bay. The foreigner thinks of Mount Fuji as the symbol of Japan, and of course it is a source of wonder and pride to most Japanese, but it doesn't get a place among the "three views."

The Inland Sea too provides more than an album of water views. It is a startlingly beautiful place—a part of the ocean captured and tamed by three of the four main islands of Japan. Along its shores cities and towns sit like spectators watching the changing patterns of reflected light. At times the sea is filled with diamonds; at times it is a mirror reflecting the blue or cloudy sky. Seldom is it tossed by storms. A vast marina for hundreds of tiny islands.

But it is not just the views that make Japan a place of water. Its abundance, its uses, and people's attitudes to it are in many ways exceptional. It often seems that the people themselves take it for granted. It is there, it is theirs. But in fact their involvement runs deep and the most simple uses of water sometimes have far greater significance than at first appears.

One sees the entrances to houses and shops being splashed with water each day, and the street outside too, to settle the dust and keep it clean. Entrance halls of traditional inns are often permanently wet from water thrown onto the paved floor. But there is more to this than just good housekeeping. It is evidence of an eye for

natural beauty, for the Japanese know that rocks and stones show themselves to best advantage when they are wet. And it is also a ritual act of purification, washing away the evil that might enter from outside.

As one travels around one accepts eagerly the watery indulgences offered along the way. There's the midsummer pleasure of a frosty glass of water and an icy-cold wet towel placed before you on arrival in any restaurant or coffee shop, however small it is, and in winter a towel so hot that one can barely hold it between thumb and forefinger for long enough to shake some of the heat out of it before wiping one's face and hands. And then there's the bath, which the Japanese love so much and spend so much time in. Psychiatrists are few in Japan and it seems unlikely that their numbers will increase so long as there are big hot baths to soak out frustrations and despair.

There are several water gods in Japan's hierarchy, but the one most unlike the water gods of other cultures is the *kappa*. Perhaps *kappa* are more water spirits than gods, for they live in large numbers in mountain streams throughout Japan. The *kappa* is a

very curious creature, standing upright, with webbed feet and hands, a tortoise shell on his back; a pixielike face grins through a duckbill, and strangest of all is the top of his head, which is concave like a basin. He is unable to survive out of water, and so when he leaves his river he takes some of it with him in the hollow of his head. Once the water dries up he dies, and so his excursions on land are brief. He is mischievous, fond of cucumbers, and so forever raiding farmers' gardens; he frequently joins up with a gang and makes war on other gangs of *kappa;* and unless appeased by priestly invocations is rather wont to grab people by the leg and pull them into the river. He has alas been known to drown children. The origins of this fantastic creature are somewhat obscure, but in many ways he is the most Japanese of the gods.

Though the Japanese are committed to water, there are few displays of national pride in the sea or in the waters of Japan, no heritage of sea songs, few tales of the sea or the waterways, no sailor heroes. The Japanese are not flamboyant people. Restraint is exercised in most things, and even when passions run high there is little evidence of it unless it is so out of hand that it explodes insanely. Perhaps this re-

straint also applies to their view of water. Yet so much of what Japan has been, is now, and will be a hundred years from now hinges on the relationship between its people and the water that surrounds them. Their life is dependent on it in the practical sense and in the inspirational sense as well. Like the *kappa*, the Japanese have water in their heads and they cannot live without it.

It seemed to us that if we were to make pictures and tell a story about water, Japan was the best place to do it. Equally it seemed that if we were to explore our feelings about the Japan we knew and wanted to know better, water was the ideal medium through which to make our journey. The result is a closer look at something we overlook most of the time. And perhaps by looking more closely at water we will get a little more joy from our encounters with it. At the same time we hope that Japan will reveal herself more fully. We will leave to other books the rounded view of Japan. That is not our purpose. We will show only one thin slice of the life of this country as we see it. But if it is a true cross section, the basic structure and the elements that go to make up the whole should be apparent.

WATER

Natural Water

For someone brought up near the sea where the surf breaks on wide golden sand beaches, as it does in California or Australia, Japan's seacoast is a great disappointment. It is not without its attractions, but its attractions are quite different. Also the Japanese attitude toward their oceans is different. To us, the sea has always represented the start of something—the beginning of the rest of the world, an inviting world waiting to be explored. To the Japanese, the sea is the opposite. It is a barrier, the end of the road, that which keeps Japan separate. It is mysterious and dangerous, and it is at one's peril that one crosses the line. Beyond it is the unknown and the undesirable.

Perhaps because of this Japan's coastline seems most real and most fascinating when the weather is bad. When a gray sky lowers to even grayer sand and steely rocks, the door is safely closed and all eyes turn inward.

The coastline is a series of battlements. Nature's own tall cliffs and heaped-up rocks, or those made by man to keep the sea away from the softer places—concrete shapes spilled along the shore like the counters of some game of chance.

It is not a coastline that invites one to kick off one's shoes. One should participate, if at all, from a discreet distance.

Beach

There are white and sandy beaches in odd corners of Japan, but they are rare. The predominant color of the beaches is gray, the predominant condition littered. Perhaps it is because the seacoast is the outer edge of Japan, almost outside it already, that the Japanese are so careless of its cleanness. Dumping waste into the sea or leaving litter on the beaches is somehow akin to putting rubbish out into the street for collection. The sea, however, seldom takes it away.

In summer the few sandy beaches near the major cities are crowded. Each Saturday and Sunday incredible numbers assemble to take to the water, and always it seems to be a record crowd. Newspaper photographers delight in showing congestion such that it is impossible to see sand for people and at times impossible to see sea for people. It is even more extraordinary that in among this dense mass of people several manage to drown themselves each weekend, and these figures are awaited with the same expectancy as the size of the record crowds who somehow didn't notice their neighbor's third rise to the surface.

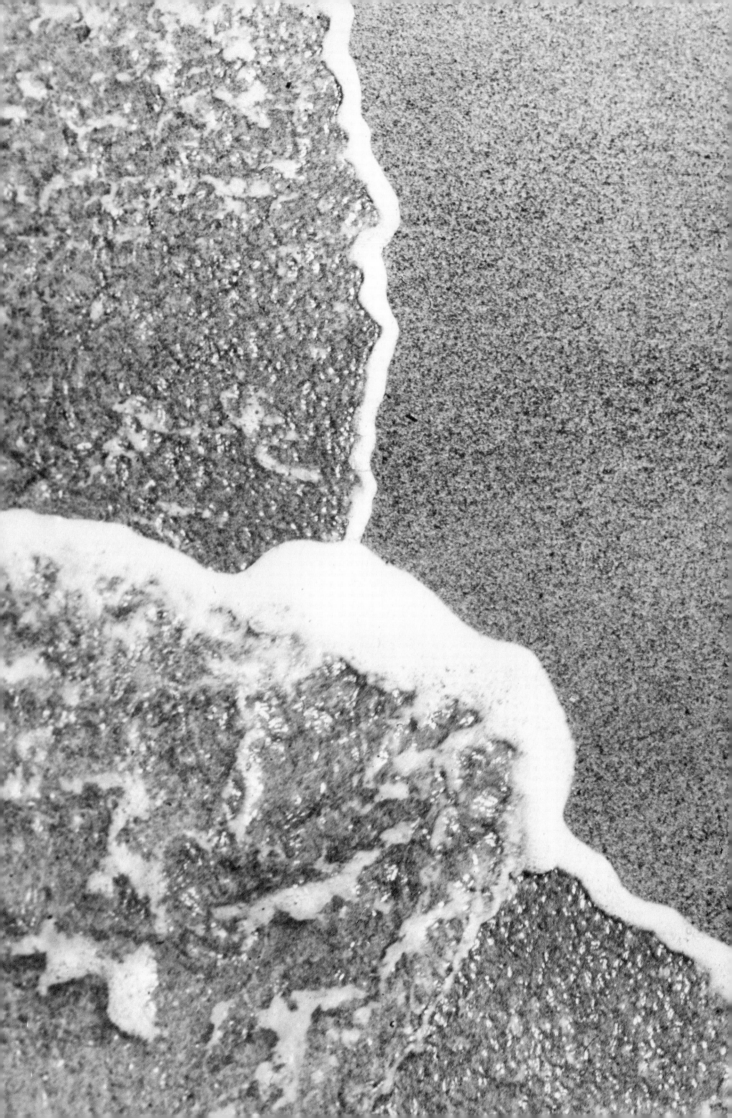

On the third Sunday of September it is announced that the swimming season is over and with a great sense of discipline nobody goes swimming any more. It is said that the reason for the end of the swimming season is the arrival of the jellyfish who, since the date is fixed several weeks ahead, must be even more disciplined than the swimmers.

For the rest of the year the beaches take on a look of desolation. The debris of the summer lingers on and the beach has the forlorn look of an unkempt garden or a sick dog. These gray, empty beaches are suddenly as unpopular as they had been popular, just a few days before, during the rush hour of the season.

River

Inland water is a different matter. It is not held at arm's length as is the sea, nor is it subject to the fickleness with which beaches are debauched and abandoned. The rivers and inland waterways of Japan are treated with a little more affection, and they are certainly the source of more enjoyment.

Japan is mostly mountains, many of them tall and snowcapped. Melting snow and rain form a web of tiny streams that unite and swell and become the rivers which flow down through the valleys until they reach the plain and, soon after, the sea. Because close on ninety percent of their journey is through the mountains, they are very busy rivers, rushing through gorges and steep valleys, constantly agitated by rocky beds, sometimes making precipitous leaps to a lower level. They are not the broad, placid rivers of the rest of Asia. They do not meander across flatlands and fan out into broad, marshy deltas. They are businesslike rivers—always in a hurry.

It is probably this aspect which the Japanese like so much. Rivers are a constant reminder that life is a progression from this to that, that present is quickly past, and that making the most of now is of paramount importance. The future has its promises, but catching the present and holding it for a moment is more important than dreaming of things to come. Such thinking is the basis of Zen. Such thinking also accounts for a large part of the country's success.

Every village, every town has its fast-running stream forced to be tidy by stone or concrete walls that limit its activity. Unfortunate though these restrictions often are, they sometimes offer a compensating prospect. Houses are built hard against these artificial banks and little Venices can be found at regular intervals along a river's course. In the older parts of the major cities the better restaurants and inns are built along the banks, and on a summer night cool breezes, the splash of water, and the sound of the *shamisen* make men forget tomorrow.

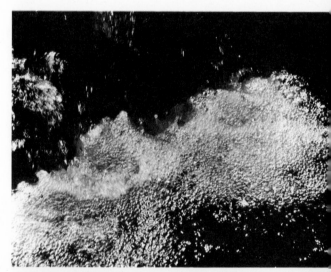

Lake

Japan's lakes are for the most part formed by
volcanic action. Their shape or their situation
is often strange and unexpected. Held firmly
in the grip of a volcano's crater, a lake looks
like an offering to the gods. A magic potion in
a bowl of earth.

Morning is the best time for lakes. Early
in the morning when the light is cold and the
air is still, the lake seems to disappear. The
water has no life of its own. Passively it re-
flects whatever is above it. Images of mountains, trees, houses are held upside down at
the lake's edge. Landscapes folded over at the
center.

At times like this, water is reduced to its
minimal state: colorless, odorless, tasteless—
yet far more mysterious than the chemistry
books would suggest. It is a mirror crowded
with images of no substance, an Alice's looking glass inviting one to slip beneath the surface of the world. And one might sink without
a ripple.

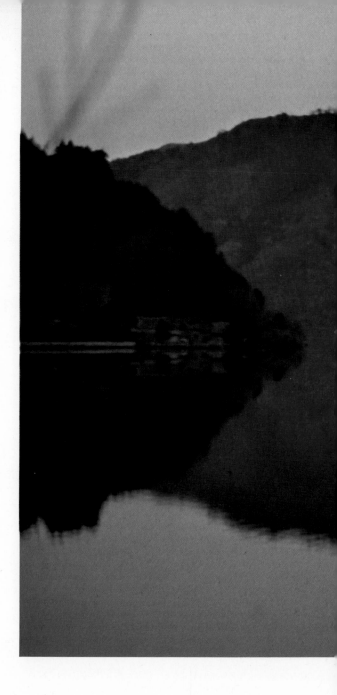

Waterfall

Waterfalls are extraordinarily generous things. They offer more than most of nature's other entertainments. They are masters of deception. They deceive the eye and the intellect.

First there is the slow motion trick. As we follow the water over the top and down the face of the fall, our eyes run ahead of it. It is necessary to backtrack constantly. The water seems to fall more slowly than it should.

Then there is the perpetual motion trick. The many tons of water that pour endlessly over the edge seem by some strange device to all go back to the top and fall down again. Of course that is exactly what happens, but the trick is to make it seem so simple. We can watch only a small part of the endless chain of evaporation, condensation, rain, river, waterfall, ocean, evaporation—but it seems as though we are seeing it all, the same water going round and round.

The cleverest trick of all belongs to the Otonashi no Taki, a waterfall near Kyoto. As the water tumbles to the rocks below, one expects to hear a roar of thunder. But this fall has turned off the sound—a silent waterfall.

Rain

When it is raining our field of vision becomes narrower, our focus shorter. Oceans and lakes and rivers disappear and the watery world becomes a place of trickles and drops and puddles. We are always inside looking out—through windows or from under umbrellas—and we can see short distances only through the falling rain.

There are many discomforts: wet socks in wet shoes, chilly water trickling down the back of the neck, water drops on glasses, the animal smell of wet wool. There is the nuisance of umbrellas, where to put them, how to close them, where to find them. Yet there are nice things too. There is an intimacy caused by rain. The world is smaller, people huddle together. Being inside looking out is very comforting. The sounds of the rain are soothing, whether beating on the roof or splashing on a broad-leafed plant or drumming in a drainpipe.

There are several rainy periods each year in Japan, but the one that is commonly known as "the rainy season" is from the beginning of June to mid-July (*tsuyu*). For six weeks the air inside as well as outside is damp, visibility is limited, and most days it drizzles. It lasts just long enough for shoes and books to go moldy. Fortunately, it is followed immediately by the hot, hot summer, which dries everything out again. In September there is another rainy period (*shūrin*) and between the two come the typhoons. In spring there is *natane*, a gentle rainy season that gets its name from the rapeseed plant whose yellow flowers come out at the same time.

The in-between rains are no more than passing showers, but the array of names given them indicates an understanding of their subtle differences: *yūdachi* (evening shower in summer), *harusame* (fine spring rain), *shigure* (winter icy rain), *samidare* (early summer rain), *niwaka-ame* (sudden rain), *kirisame* (drizzle), *konuka-ame* (misty rain), *ō-ame* (downpour).

The Japanese collect rain experiences as they might collect different colors or different values of a postage stamp. To have seen a particular garden or a particular view in different seasons or under snow or in the rain adds to one's appreciation of it. Listed among the most beautiful sights or tourist attractions of Japan one frequently finds "such and such a place *in the rain.*" Rain is natural and therefore the experience of it should be sought out and enjoyed.

The Japanese have a soft spot for the world with a wet face.

Reflections

The world of water is a kindly place.
With their rough edges rubbed off, the
    ferroconcrete forests wave freely in the
    gentle breeze.
In a slow dissolve of stone and steel
    commercial giants fall and ancient
    monuments decline.

Upturned this melting world would be a
    nightmare trip.
And yet we find the insubstantial nature of
    the image soothing
Safe in our knowledge that rock-hard realities
    are anchored to the shore.

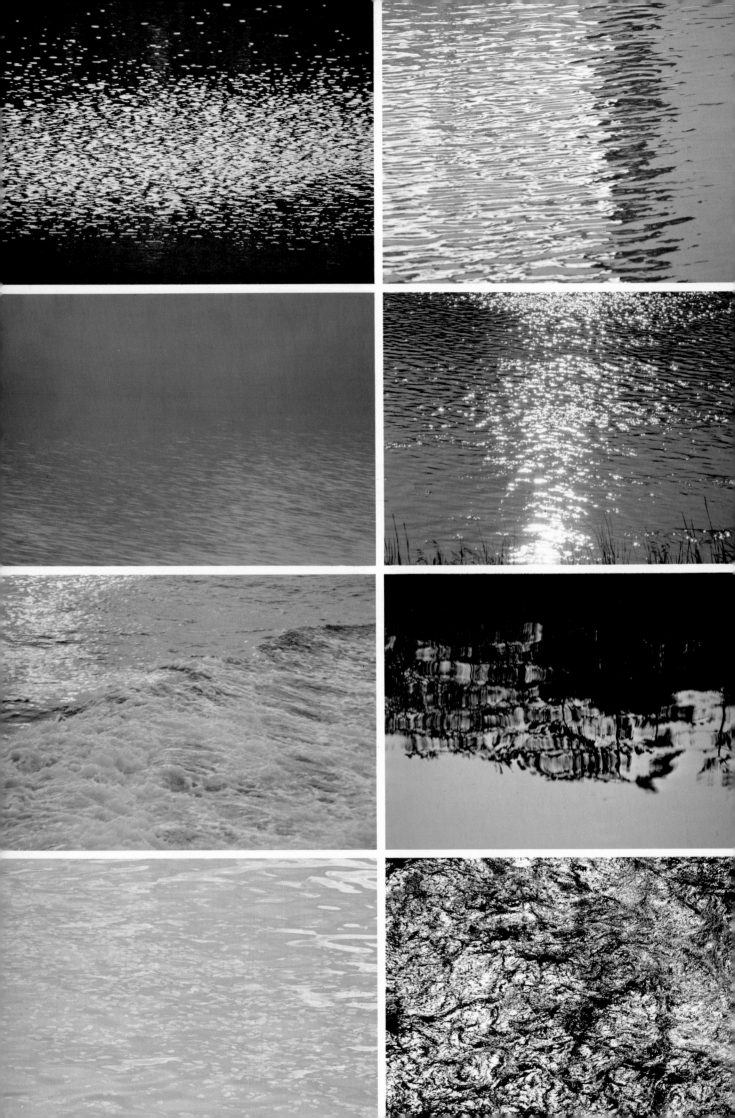

Ritual
Water

The diversity of water rituals in Japan is quite phenomenal. The ways in which water is used, and the ends sought, are numerous. One can find somewhere in Japan a water ritual to provide the relief or the assurance desired for almost any event or eventuality in one's life. An easy birth, a healthy baby, recovery from illness, success in an examination or in a new job, a propitious outcome to moving house, more money, good eyesight, longevity, peace, wisdom, and revelation—each of these can be had by the proper use of the proper water.

Ritual water works in two ways—it gives and it takes away. It gives health, wealth, wisdom because of its sacred origins or its blessed condition. It takes away evil, bad luck, or the spiritual grime of daily life by virtue of its purity or its simple cleansing properties.

How water became so central a part of religious practices in Japan is open to some doubt. Several explanations can be offered, but all stem from one undeniable fact of Japan's history—the extraordinary oneness with nature that seems always to have been a facet of the Japanese psyche. The gods of ancient Japan were nature gods. The trees, the earth, the sky, the rivers were the homes of the gods or were themselves gods. Immersing oneself in a river was perhaps the most intimate contact one could have with a deity, and this symbolic consummation of the man-god relationship may be the origin of the earliest water rituals. Shrines were built in places of natural beauty, where most often there was a river, a spring, or a waterfall. Water may have become associated with the religious performances within the shrine simply because it was there. Whatever the reasons, the use of water in purification rituals has been an essential part of Shintō, the native religion of Japan, since before recorded history.

Not far inside the gate of every shrine is a *mitarashi*—a stone basin of water used by worshipers to cleanse their mouths and hands before entering the inner precincts of the shrine.

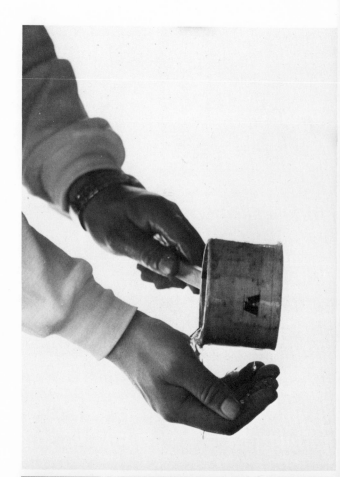

Mitarashi

O-Bon

Bon is a season of bonuses and gifts, of dances and dead souls floating across the water to paradise.

The *bon* festivals held throughout the country in midsummer are happy as well as holy occasions. On the first night of *o-bon* the spirits of the dead return to stay with their families for three days, but at the end of this time they must leave. To mark their departure, lanterns symbolizing the souls of the dead are launched into lake or stream to float out toward the land of the lotuses and the waiting smiling Amida Buddha.

Crowds come to watch these journeys of strangers' souls. Boats are rowed into the middle of the lake and lanterns are carefully set down into the water. The hot winds of summer make the journeys perilous. Reflections of lights shatter into colored pieces, and swaying lotus leaves beckon as the frail craft carry their burning cargo wherever the winds direct them. Only the widows and the pale men notice the lanterns that capsize at sea or become stranded on the shore.

The dead have gone and the crowds move on, lured by the pounding of the drum at the top of the tower, to join in the festive dance. Round and round the tower the living dance their circle until the heat of their bodies or of their spirits leads them away into the night.

Hiruga

On the 15th of January each year about two million young men and women come of age (during the previous twelve months they have reached the age of twenty). A public holiday signifies the importance of this day, and throughout Japan there are coming of age ceremonies and celebrations. Pretty girls parade in lollypop kimono, all pink and aqua blue, and young men strut somewhat, full of bonhomie and the obligation to prove something.

In the small fishing village of Hiruga, on the Japan Sea coast, the 15th of January is a double festival. It is Hiruga's once a year day, and the whole village turns out to watch the annual tug of war. In theory two teams plunge into the freezing water of the canal that leads into the sea and, in a demonstration of strength, break a rope of plaited rice stalks that has been stretched from bank to bank and floats on the surface of the water. The ritual breaking of the rope ensures a good harvest from the fields and the sea.

The strength and virility of the men of the village is shored up by large quantities of sakè, and it is not until a sufficient state of numbness has been reached that the contestants are ready to plunge into the water and attack the rope. Meanwhile the crowd has been waiting with remarkable patience, frozen by the wind and not fortified by sakè, undergoing their own endurance test. Eventually the contestants appear, ruddy with fortification, and clearly not focusing. They fall rather than plunge into the water and set about the task of breaking the rope. What happens does not seem like a tug of war. Rather, the rope is unpicked. Handfuls of rice stalks are torn from it bit by bit until eventually it comes apart. If there ever were two teams, it is never apparent. The crowd is happy. The spectacle is over. The victors float with the rope, now

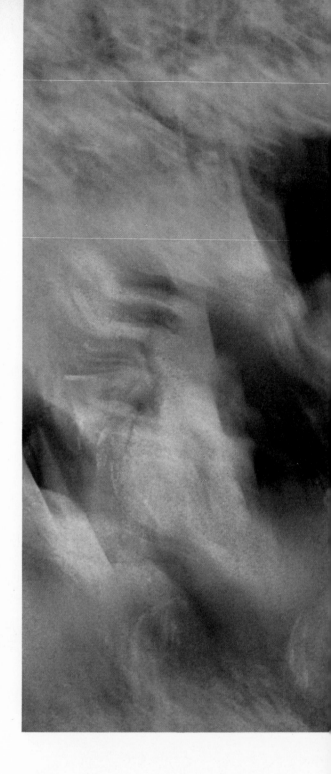

in two pieces on the tide, to the end of the breakwater. They emerge from the sea, still pink and proud of their achievements. The pretty girls give them a measure of rice (isshō-masu) as their reward. The village, having proved itself, goes home to get warm. No doubt there will be many toasts to the good harvest they will have and to the young men and women who have come of age that day.

Fire

The character for water (水) is painted or carved on the roof of a house to protect it from fire. A roof with water on it will not burn.

Birth

The water god (*suijin-sama*) supervises the birth of babies. To ensure an easy delivery, an offering is made at a shrine dedicated to him.

Death

To honor the dead, tombstones are washed with water when family or friends visit a cemetery.

Initiation

Halfway up the mountain it is still winter. The snow has gone and the trees are slowly coming alive again, but the air still bites at the ears and the earth is damp and cold. It is necessary to move one's toes to keep the circulation going.

The waterfall is to be opened today. According to the calendar of events of the Yakuō-in temple, it has been closed for the winter. The waterfall is not a tourist attraction but an integral part of religious observances at this temple. It is here beneath the waterfall that the priests and the devout who come here put themselves and their beliefs to a severe test.

Led by the chief priest, the willing victims of this attack one by one take their turn at standing or sitting under the falling water. Banging away at their heads or shoulders, the steely spikes of icy water force out the evil housed within these brave bodies. The result is a dazed euphoria. The body is clean. The mind is pure. The world has been made a sweeter, better place.

What dreadful deeds or thoughts could need such purging? One suspects they are the most innocent of minds and bodies that are punished by this icy pounding.

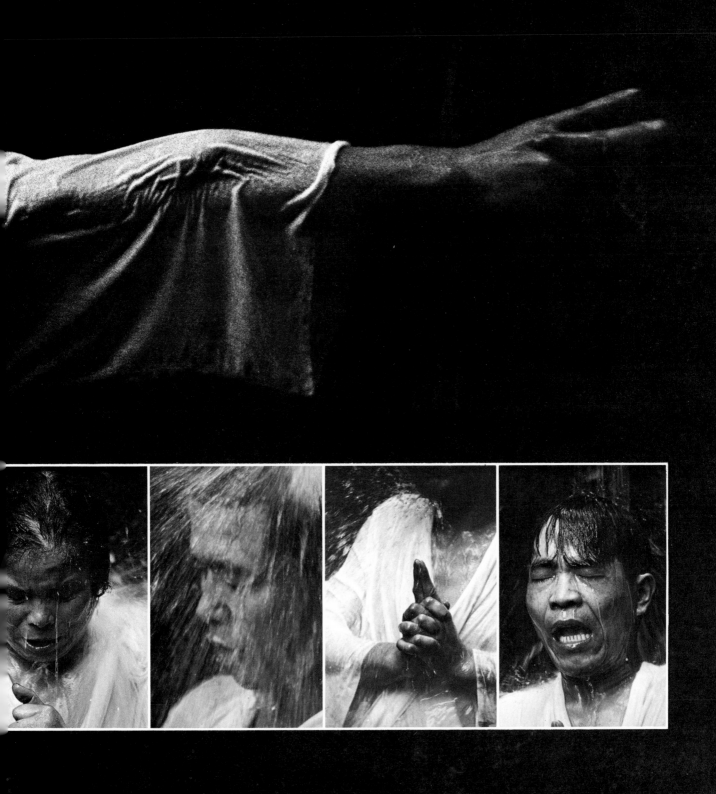

Boat Festival

In the Heian period, when the court in Kyoto was more concerned with writing poetry and moon viewing than with ruling and warring, a popular diversion was the boating party. The ultimate was a private party of a dozen or so of one's closest or most influential friends on one's own lake, but the public displays were the more frequent. One needed considerable rank to warrant a place in one of the boats when the imperial party drifted down the river at Arashiyama looking at the changing colors of the autumn leaves and watching the entertainments. The flotilla comprised perhaps twenty or thirty boats, several of which carried troupes of entertainers—musicians, singers, dancers, actors—who performed on the water.

They were splendid processions and rather noisy ones too. The gossip and laughter of court ladies rippled from boat to boat, and men, with robust voices, challenged their opponents in poetry contests. Arashiyama must be the most described and most eulogized place in all Japan.

A thousand years later at the annual boat festival at Arashiyama these cultivated outings are reenacted. The progress of the boats is probably much the same as it always was, but the crowds who come to watch are bigger—and braver. They join the procession in their little boats, and the rowers flirt with the "court ladies." The young people of Kyoto who are filling in for the lords and ladies of the court gossip about dates and discos, boyfriends and hairstyles. The idiom has changed, but the conversation is probably little different from that of the pink Heian days.

Sensual Water

What is so good about a bath? Stimulation, warmth, comfort, relaxation? All of these and more:

There's the brisk rubbing with a loose woven towel, a sort of self-inflicted birch-beating, until pinkness brightens dull skin which, tingling, seems to free itself from the flesh beneath. It comes alive doubly aware of warmth and cold and the significance of touch.

And washing away the soap by dipping water from the bath and throwing it at oneself. A solid slap of wetness that leaves the eyes bound tight with bands of hair layered out like seaweed caught in a strong current.

And the water, intimate as the skin itself, clings and caresses. Rivulets as tentative as a sigh finger their way along a thigh or circumnavigate a glistening breast, lingering in dewy crevices.

And then the getting into the too hot water, easing the body gently down the side of the bath until only the head protrudes and bottom touches bottom. And staying still for a few minutes to become accustomed to the heat because each movement seems to raise the temperature several degrees.

And after a while to move about a bit and let the water take the weight out of the body, massaging it with fingers of opposing force, and rocking it toward a state of sleep.

And then as relaxation spreads its tendrils through the brain to sit on a wooden stool or the cold tiles and cool off, mopping up the larger drops of water with the wrung-out towel and letting the rest rise from the body as a cloud of steam.

Apart from sex, there is no bodily encounter so sensual as the bath.

And no bath as fulfilling as the Japanese bath.

Furoya

Japan is one of the few places left where the bath is a social event. Elsewhere civilization has destroyed man's primitive urge to splash and play and talk and laugh and enjoy the water that cleans the body. Bathing has become a closet act, a secret and solitary indulgence or a pleasureless routine. Not so in the bathhouse.

Alone, a bath may take minutes; with one's family or friends, it may take an hour or more. In the big bath one can soak and talk with a dozen people. One can play with the children. Even watch television. Stripped of clothes and pretenses, it's a return to square one each time one enters a bathhouse. It is difficult to be important or arrogant or superior if you are naked.

Economic success, convenience—even modesty—will eventually close the public bathhouses. It is to be hoped that the thousands of *onsen* and resort hotels will keep alive the love of the big bath.

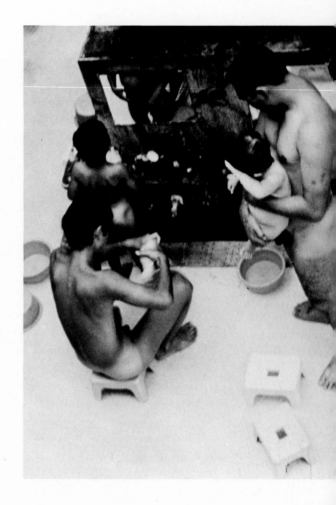

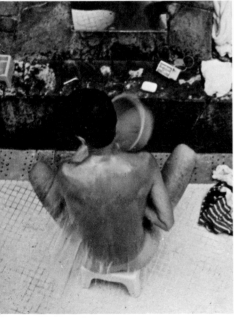

Onsen

There are very few places in Japan where one is not within twenty miles or so of an *onsen* (hot spring). Around the source of the hot water one finds a scattering of hotels ranging from small, intimate inns whose reputations stem from the quality of their service and their food and perhaps the uniqueness of their appearance or their location to the giant thousand-room hotels whose reputations depend chiefly on the size of their baths (at least three of these hotels claim to have the biggest bath in the world).

To a Westerner the idea of visiting a spa "to take the waters" has strong geriatric associations. In Japan, though all sorts of therapeutic benefits are claimed for the waters, they have a very general appeal. And in the larger hotels the bath itself is designed to ensure this. The baths are pleasure domes. At night, when they are most crowded, artificial stars twinkle in the ceiling among the angels suspended on wires from heaven, or strings of colored lights and balloons turn them into fairgrounds. Most have vast indoor gardens, and from the bath one can see papayas and bunches of bananas ripening on the trees. There are statues and urns and occasional attempts at art that lend the look of Italian gardens.

In this extravagant setting one can choose one's water. There is purified water, salt water, mineral water, hormone water—almost any kind of water that nature offers or man has manufactured to satisfy whatever needs need satisfaction. There is clear water, muddy water, colored water. Temperatures range from icy to scalding. There is still water, bubbling water, surging water. One can cure rheumatism, improve sexual performance (by sitting in a heart filled with hormone water), smooth the skin, strengthen bones. Or one can just relax and enjoy the sensations.

Up to one's neck in hot water, the troubles of the world seep away. One escapes from import duties, export quotas, the bank rate, new elections, or the railway strike. One escapes from *my job, my home, my car, my family*. In two strokes one can swim to the other side, relaxed and free, naked in a hot sea.

Sometimes the hot water is not brought indoors, but is left where it bubbles out of the ground into a rocky pool. There, under a blue sky or in the moonlight, small groups of naked people soak in a hot bath. Sometimes a lean-to and a few bamboo blinds afford a little privacy, but most often the outdoor bath is unashamedly in the open, for that's what it's all about, the freedom and fun of enjoying water and rocks and trees and people just as nature made them.

Even in the snow.

In an early morning river
 a consumers union
 holds communion

People travel hundreds of miles and office parties set off at noon on Saturday and stay at a hotel for a weekend, just to take a bath.

Awesome Water

That the earth is still soft in the center seems little more than a plausible theory as we tread the crusty surface (or the concrete with which we've covered it). We give it little thought. It does nothing to shape our lives. Then one day the earth lets off steam to show us that inside there's a pot of trouble brewing. A volcano erupts, an earthquake breaks the crust, a fissure appears that leads down into the soft core providing a passage through which unthinkable horrors can escape.

Water accumulates under the surface of the earth. At points where the crust is thin, the molten center heats it. If water or steam escapes from this underground teakettle, it appears benignly as a hot spring or in more sinister form as a "hell." Hell (*jigoku* in Japanese) is the name given to a pool of boiling mud or water. There are many in Japan, constant reminders that our confidence in having our feet firmly planted on solid earth is perhaps ill-founded.

When the earth was a million years younger, its surface was pockmarked by a myriad of such hellholes. But as the millennia passed, many of the sores healed. A million years from now the cure will be complete, and the inhabitants of the earth will be denied the morbid thrill we get from gazing for a few moments into hell.

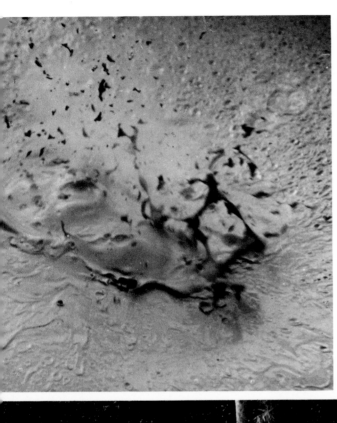

Hells

In Beppu on Kyūshū there exist side by side examples of almost all the different kinds of *jigoku* that can be seen in Japan. A tour of them all gives one in a short space of time a fairly comprehensive view. But it is disappointing and strikes a note of illogic that one has to pay admission to hell.

Each bubbling or steaming pond is charged for separately, although a multiple ticket will get you each one at a cheaper price, with an alligator farm thrown in. Each is surrounded by a dozen souvenir stalls and, of course, hundreds of people. Despite all these distractions, the awe is still there.

Depending on the mineral deposits in the surrounding rocks, the steaming pools take on the colors of the salts dissolved in them. Iron deposits make water red; copper, blue; calcium, white. The devil's paint pots.

But Beppu lacks the tinge of desolation that one feels while watching water bubbling in the crater of a volcano, or breathing the sulfurous stench exuded from a patch of boiling mud on a bleak hillside. The hells of Beppu are domesticated.

Whirlpool

The Inland Sea has four entrances—four narrow channels between large islands. One of these is the Straits of Naruto. Here, when the tide turns, opposing currents collide and the water swirls in great circles. Caught in one of these vortexes, a small craft can be sucked under, stripped of its contents, and spat out again like unwanted bones.

When the weather is bad and the waves run high the place should be avoided, but when the waters are calm the tourists come in little boats to watch the whirlpools swallowing the sea.

Swamps

Swamps are cold, dark places full of bats and snakes. Owls hoot on moonlight nights and vampires move about in the shadows. Or so the archetypal image goes. But there are also sunny swamps. Fields of golden reeds moving in a gentle breeze and patches of water reflecting a clear blue sky are hardly the setting for a horror movie. Nonetheless there is something out of step with the accepted order to find vast areas of lush grassland forever submerged. Somehow it is easier to accept the dank, festering place our imagination expects a swamp to be.

In the swamps of Oze one walks for miles on trunks of trees laid end to end in the shallows. On either side of this log path stretch wide meadows of water. One is surrounded by a sunken landscape. And through the water strange currents flow, underwater rivers moving like the great ocean currents. Curving this way and that way through the quivering undergrowth, they carve out odd patterns in the swamp.

Thunderstorm

Spectacular thunderstorms are not all that frequent in Japan. They come in summer, and there is something theatrical about the way they do it. Within moments of their entrance they have taken center stage and in no time at all they have shown us all their art. We judge their performance as we do an actor's: With many we become quickly bored; they offer nothing new, the same old gestures, the same superficiality. With some we are cowed by their virtuosity.

From the first rumble of thunder the great ones make us stop whatever we are doing and take notice. The sky quickly fills with dark clouds and the next few minutes is like watching a *sumi-e* painter at work. Watery black ink applied stroke after stroke intensifies gray washes until dense black mountains loom in the sky. In the middle of the day the sky cannot get much darker. And then the street lights come on as though they too have been convinced and moved to action by the drama. Now the wind starts up—not a slow crescendo but a sudden onslaught that lifts anything resting lightly on the earth and throws it through the air. The trees react with a screech and an occasional crack as a branch, unbraced and caught unaware, is split from its trunk. Iron buckles, timbers creak, ropes slap at the sides of flagpoles, and all around there are noises like drums and gunshot. And then the sky is white with fire and adults count the seconds between the lightning and the thunder and children hide their navels (Kaminari-sama, the god of thunder, steals navels).

And then the rain.

For those first drops, "rain" seems an inappropriate word. The drops of water are thick and solid and leave splash marks the size of saucers. They fall heavily and noisily and for a long time. The drama in the skies, however, is almost over. Everything becomes a uniform dark gray. The air is filled with water, and soon the rain comes down in earnest the way it should. The performance is really over once the rain starts in. People stand straight again. They take cover or go home or back to the television. The remaining cracks of thunder have lost their impact.

Typhoon

Thunderstorms frighten children; typhoons kill people. They are not entertainments.

During the period from July to September about thirty or so typhoons are born in the South China Sea. They move great distances and they take a long time to make their journey. Of the thirty, about half head toward Japan. Fewer than ten cross the coast. Most are spent. Some are still in their prime.

Several days before the arrival of a typhoon, its presence is announced. Its movements are followed by many quietly anxious people. There are maps in newspapers and on television, and its hour-by-hour progress is broadcast over the radio. Westerners give them names—Typhoon Claire, Typhoon Edna— perhaps in an attempt to make them less sinister. The Japanese give them numbers. They do not try to make friends with potential treachery.

As much as a day before the arrival of a typhoon, the trees begin to move uncertainly. Especially the willows. They tremble. The wind stays light but restless, and it is then that one begins to listen closely to the broadcasts. The main topic now is the point at which the typhoon will hit the coast, for often they change direction at the last moment. When a likely point of impact is announced, people calmly go about securing their personal possessions or the things for which they are responsible. In the coastal villages boats are beached and tied down. Houses are shuttered. Extra props are given to preferred trees.

In the typhoon areas many precautions have been taken on a permanent basis, so it is usually a simple matter of putting a predetermined plan into action. For the larger buildings (hotels, office buildings, factories), it may mean some broken glass or at worst a section of roofing blown off. But for the householder, it can mean the end of everything. No home. No family. Whenever a typhoon hits, there are

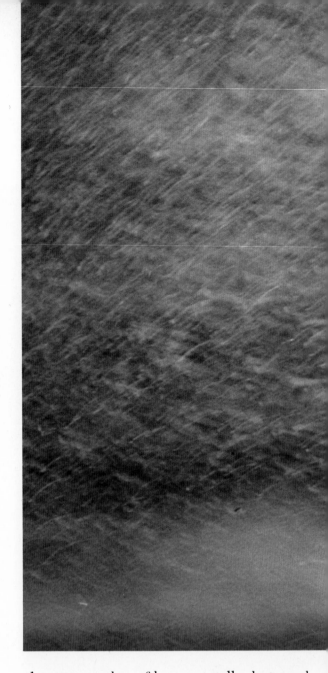

always a number of houses totally destroyed (on some occasions the number has been in the thousands). Invariably there is some loss of life. The hazards to the individual are numerous. Houses collapse, building materials are blown through the air, power lines fall, waves crash across breakwaters and sweep the unsuspecting into the sea. People have even been blown into the sea. Near the center of a typhoon, winds may reach velocities of 100 to 150 miles per hour.

There is, however very little panic. There is adequate warning. Precautions are taken. One can only wait and be prepared to face tomorrow. For most, tomorrow will be a big cleanup and a restoration of calm. For a few it will be a continuing nightmare of irreplaceable loss.

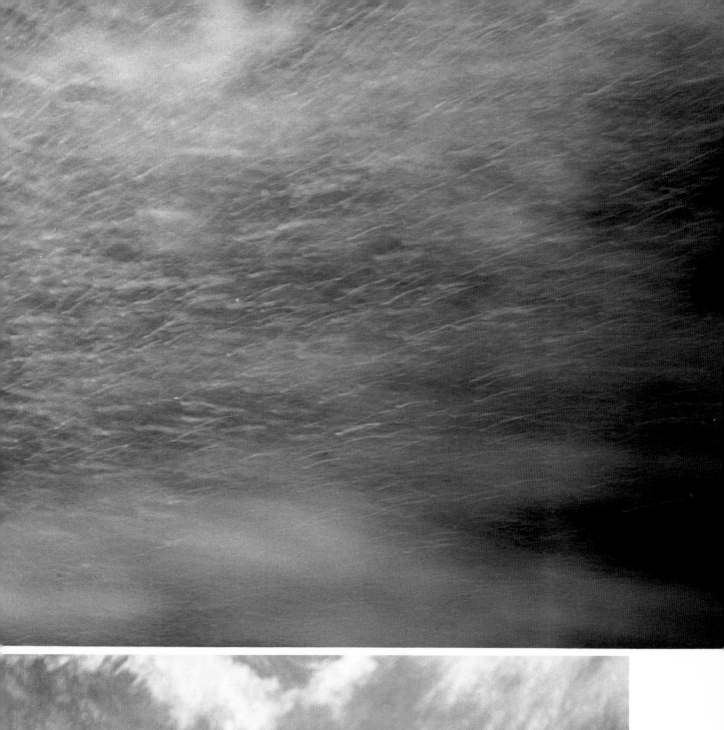

Historical
Water

Page. 41.

JAPONÆ
ac
TERRÆ IESSONIS
Novissima Descriptio
Robᵗ. Morden

COREA I.

Oqui I.

Taquixima

I. d' Ladrones al
Qualpaerts

Foqui
Nagata
Simonisicci
Amangachi
Camenosacci
Binga

A
B

Kikero
Oun emari
Fiſen
Nangasacqui
Cane goxuma

BUNGO I.
Straite of Deimen

I. Firando

Gotto I.

Arima

Meacexima

Tanaixima

TONSAI.

Ciko

In the seventh generation of the gods came Izanami and Izanagi. From the Bridge of Heaven, one day, they stirred up the waters of the ocean with a spear. When they withdrew it, a single drop of water clung to it. This they shook free and it fell back into the ocean to become one of the islands of Japan. Thus Japan was born of water.

Izanami and Izanagi came down from the heavens and after a remarkable game of chasing round the island, Izanami gave birth to the other islands and to a sizable family of gods. As she gave birth to the last of these, the god of fire, she was burned so badly that she died. The distraught Izanagi journeyed to the land of the dead to bring her back. He seems to have failed, for he returned without her. But since he had come in contact with the dead, it was necessary on his return to purify himself. This he did by washing in the ocean. In washing his left eye he created Amaterasu, the sun goddess. In washing his right eye he created the moon god. In washing his nose he created the storm god, Susano-o, who is often likened to the Greek god Poseidon since he lived in the sea from whence storms were born.

Amaterasu and her brother Susano-o were an ill-tempered pair who fought constantly. On one occasion he made her so angry that she hid herself in a cave, thus plunging the world into darkness. In order to entice her out, an erotic show was staged for a gathering of gods, whose rowdy reception of the event was too much for Amaterasu's curiosity. She peered out from the cave and saw herself reflected in a mirror that had been pointed in her direction. And such was her astonishment or delight at seeing herself that she emerged from the cave. Light was restored.

The cave where Amaterasu hid herself is said to be the one at Futamigaura on the Ise Peninsula. Just offshore are two rocks that represent Izanami and Izanagi. They are tied together by a rope made of rice stalks. Nearby are the Ise Grand Shrines, where one of the imperial regalia—the mirror used to lure Amaterasu from her hiding place—is enshrined. These are the holiest of places in Japan, and the area bristles with gods and cures and curses. It has an authenticity built of centuries of unquestioning belief in the mythology it celebrates.

After the cave incident and because of his impossible behavior, Susano-o was banished by the other gods. Prior to all this, however, and between feuds, he and his sister Amaterasu produced eight children, the eldest of whom was the first of the unbroken line of emperors of Japan. Amaterasu's great-great-grandson, in keeping with the strange matrimonial habits of his forebears, married his aunt and fathered Jimmu Tennō.

It is here that mythology and history merge. It is thought that Jimmu Tennō was indeed a historical figure, probably a powerful chieftain who subjugated and united a considerable part of the country. It is suggested that his reign began in the year 660 B.C.; it is also suggested that he was a contemporary of Julius Caesar. Because of the lack of records, Japanese history cannot truly be said to begin until about 500 A.D. and so the existence or otherwise of Jimmu Tennō, his ancestors, and many of his successors will remain forever a matter of scholarly speculation.

Dannoura

In every country's history there are major turning points. In the history of Japan, most of the turning points have been connected with the sea.

In the year 1185 the decisive sea battle at Dannoura marked such a turning point. It was the final stroke in more than two hundred years of rivalry between the two most powerful families in Japan. The Minamoto and the Taira had each won and lost the favor of the imperial court in Kyoto several times. Each had experienced both victory and defeat in the series of bloody battles they had fought to gain supremacy. From 1150 the Taira had dominated. Their leader, Kiyomori, had his daughter married to the emperor, and the son of this marriage, Antoku, became emperor as an infant in 1180.

That same year the Minamoto rose in rebellion against the Taira. Kiyomori, the Taira leader, died in the following year, and the Taira power began to weaken. Kiyomori's family, including the infant Antoku, fled to the south and finally took refuge on the Taira ships. The Taira fleet was later engaged by the Minamoto forces led by Yoshitsune and the ship carrying the precious imperial cargo was sunk along with the rest. For the Taira it was a total and final defeat. On board were the imperial regalia—mirror, sword, and jewels. It is reported that Kiyomori's widow took the sword and Antoku in her arms and threw herself into the sea, where they drowned. The sword was never recovered.

The Battle of Dannoura stands as a monument in Japanese history—the end of an era of shifting-sand politics, of warring families, of epic heroes; the beginning of military rule and of the highly organized feudal state that was to stabilize and unite the country for the next seven hundred years.

Kamikaze

By the latter half of the thirteenth century Japan had experienced a great deal of civil strife, but she had never experienced a threat from outside until Kublai Khan sent his ships to invade her. Kublai, the grandson of the great Genghis Khan, ruled an empire that stretched from Eastern Europe to Korea. He had sent ambassadors to Japan to demand tribute, but the ambassadors had been turned away. In 1274 he sent a fleet of ships and a landing was made on Kyūshū, the southern-most island. A storm arose, however, and the invaders returned to their ships and took them to safer waters. The attempted invasion achieved little for the Mongols, but on the assumption that the complacency of the Japanese had been shaken, ambassadors were again sent to demand acquiescence. The reply sent to Kublai Khan was the severed heads of his ambassadors.

In 1281 Kublai Khan sent another invasion fleet. This time there were several hundred ships and again a landing was made on Kyūshū. But the invaders, intent on penetrating the Japanese defenses, failed to anticipate one of the hazards of the season. It was summer and so it was not surprising to the Japanese when the air was filled with the first signs of an approaching typhoon. First there was the vacuum stillness and then the slow but insistent building of clouds, wind, and rain. Soon the full force of the typhoon hit, and an invasion that might well have succeeded was turned into a cataclysm. The Mongol fleet was totally destroyed. Those of their soldiers who were not drowned were quickly despatched by the Japanese. It was an overwhelming defeat.

The typhoon was given the name *kamikaze* (divine wind), for it was said that it was the work of the gods. Later the priests claimed recompense from the state since they had prayed so successfully. The name has become well known to the Western world, for it was used again when the need for divine intervention was great. The suicide squads who crashed their bomb-laden planes on enemy ships during the Pacific War were also given the name Kamikaze.

Castles

The use of moats as a defense against attackers was a common practice in Japan and dates as far back as the seventh century. But it was not until the sixteenth and seventeenth centuries that most of Japan's great castles were built. A moat, or more often a series of moats, surrounded the castle compound, and together with massive stone walls made these fortresses impenetrable. The only way a castle could be taken was by siege.

Most castles were well prepared to repel an enemy force at any point from the outer walls to the central tower, but there was seldom any fighting within the compound. Once a castle was besieged there was no possibility of victory unless help could be mustered from outside, and when no help came the siege often ended with the lord of the castle setting fire to the main tower—the symbol of his power—and suiciding within its burning walls.

Under Toyotomi Hideyoshi, Japan had been unified and ruled with an iron hand. At his death in 1598, Hideyoshi named Tokugawa Ieyasu as guardian of his son Hideyori and one of the regents of Japan until Hideyori came of age. Hideyori lived in Osaka Castle, which his father had built and which was reputed to be the most unassailable castle in all Japan. Ieyasu, who was determined to maintain the unity Hideyoshi had established, soon made enemies who then gathered around Hideyori.

In 1614, on the pretext of suppressing an insurrection, Ieyasu attacked the castle at Osaka. The castle was indeed impregnable and soon he resorted to a siege. When at length a peace was made, Ieyasu withdrew his forces and headed back toward Edo (modern Tokyo). Hideyori's men then undertook to fulfill one of the stipulations of the peace agreement— the filling in of the outer moat. The work was hardly underway when Ieyasu and his army returned, crossed the useless moat, and with some help from inside, took the castle. With the fall of Osaka Castle the authority of the Tokugawa shogunate, which stayed in power for 260 years, was firmly established.

The young Hideyori killed himself in his tower.

Black Ships

By 1639, a series of decrees had been issued by the government of Tokugawa Ieyasu forbidding Japanese citizens to travel to foreign countries and limiting the size of ships so that travel from Japan became impossible anyhow. All ports were closed to foreign vessels with the exception of Nagasaki (specifically, the island of Deshima in Nagasaki Bay), which was open to Dutch and Chinese traders only. In effect, Japan was sealed off from the rest of the world. Japan stayed closed for 230 years.

Only an island country with tight internal control could adopt such an isolationist policy so successfully. The sea prevented outward movement. Preoccupations elsewhere prevented the other world traders (other than the Dutch that is) from attempting to break the barrier. On rare occasions foreign ships would appear off the coast. No doubt they aroused curiosity, but they were never given permission to land and they never attempted to do so illegally and so they were of little concern to government or citizen. At the beginning of the nineteenth century, when the East was becoming the new focus of interest, foreign ships appeared more frequently. Their demands for the right to land became stronger. They were still ignored.

On the 8th of July, 1853, four black ships appeared off the coast at Uraga in Tokyo Bay. They were large ships, they were very black ships. Their commander made the strongest demands yet. He carried a letter from the President of the United States of America which he insisted be officially received by the government. He was told to submit the communication through the Dutch at Nagasaki. But he didn't go away. The black ships loomed off the coast looking larger and blacker. There were no procedures for coping with this situation.

Tales of the black ships spread throughout the country. In Kyoto, stories circulated of 100 ships and 100,000 men. Attack seemed almost certain. In an atmosphere of panic and confusion, the letter was finally accepted and signed for, and it was agreed that its contents would be considered. The letter demanded the opening of ports to American ships, agreements for the proper care and return of stranded seamen, and so on. The once-powerful military government took the unprecedented step of consulting all the lords of the various provinces and even the imperial court, something that had not been done for centuries. Many of the lords and the court said NO. Commander Perry of the black ships said he would return.

The debate continued. There was much talk of defense. Temple bells would be melted down to make cannon. Samurai would be retrained in the new martial arts. The integrity of a closed Japan would be maintained.

By the time Perry returned the next year, the Japanese had realized that the task of defending so large a coastline was impossible without a navy to attack marauders at sea. Perry was told that an agreement could be reached. Six weeks later the seal was broken and Japan's ports were one by one opened to the ships of the world. Shimoda first, then Hakodate. And after them came names like Kobe, Kure, Yokohama, Yokkaichi, all now regular calls on the Eastern trade routes.

An Imperial Navy

The growth of the Japanese navy during the late 1880s and its moments of glory at the turn of the century put fear into the hearts of the Chinese officials in Peking, caused a monumental loss of face in Czarist St. Petersburg, and left the other of the world's capitals openmouthed with wonder. How a nonseafaring nation could become one of the world's major sea powers (perhaps second to Great Britain) in such a short space of time was to most observers a total mystery. Along with the achievements came unexpected displays of gallantry and good manners that were even more amazing.

In 1885 Japan and China made a declaration in which each assured the independence of Korea (an assurance given at regular intervals in between numerous takeovers by both governments). In 1894 Chinese troops moved into Korea to quell a rebellion. Their numbers were considered excessive by the Japanese government. In July 1894 the Japanese sank a ship bearing more Chinese soldiers to Korea. The Chinese sent a squadron to do battle with the Japanese navy, which at the time was regarded as just a rather patchy collection of ships.

But at the mouth of the Yalu River, the Japanese won a surprise victory. After landing in Korea, they advanced into China and took Port Arthur, the northern fortress that guarded access to Peking. Later, the southern fortress, Weihaiwei, was captured, and the Chinese capital was at the mercy of the invader.

After the fall of Weihaiwei, the Chinese naval commander, Vice-Admiral Ting, committed suicide. The Japanese commander returned to the Chinese one of their captured ships so that Admiral Ting might be carried to his resting place in one of his own vessels. The ship's guns were left intact so that she might fire the customary salute. When the body was brought on board, the victors filed past the coffin and respectfully saluted their dead enemy. As the ship sailed, the Japanese squadron lined up in the harbor and victory flags were dipped and the ships' bands played funeral marches.

By the end of the century Russia had become the threat that China had been a few years earlier. Russia's Trans-Siberian Railway was almost complete. Her presence in Korea and her military occupation of Manchuria led her to boast that she was now mistress of the Far East. Japan started negotiating with Russia over their conflict of interest in Korea and demanded the removal of Russian forces from the area. Negotiations broke down and on February 6, 1904, Japan severed diplomatic relations with Russia. On February 9, Japan sank three battleships, five cruisers, and a gunboat of the Russian fleet. On February 10, Japan declared war.

One of the few Japanese ships lost in the early stages of the Russian War was the transport ship Kinshu Maru. The troops on board refused to abandon ship, and as she sank they continued to fire on the attacker until they were covered by the waves. All officers on board committed suicide. It was a bizarre event in naval history but a significant one, for this transfer of the samurai code to the sea was to be the hallmark of the Imperial Japanese Navy until its dissolution in 1945.

After several months of fighting, attention was again centered on Port Arthur. The area now was occupied by the Russians, but in July 1904 the Japanese army began to capture the surrounding forts. In early May the Japanese navy had closed the harbor mouth by sinking a number of merchant ships that had been purchased and moved to the site for this purpose. The siege of Port Arthur was maintained until the year end. On January 2, 1905, the Russians surrendered.

The war, however, was not over. The Russian army was still in control of Manchuria and a Russian fleet had set sail from the Baltic in October. By the time the Russian ships arrived in Japanese waters eight months later, the Japanese navy was waiting. The Japanese had chosen the spot where the two navies would meet—the Straits of Tsushima. On May 27, 1905, the Russian fleet was almost totally destroyed. The world had followed with great interest the progress of the Russian armada and learned with astonishment of its sudden annihilation.

From that moment, Japan was a major sea power.

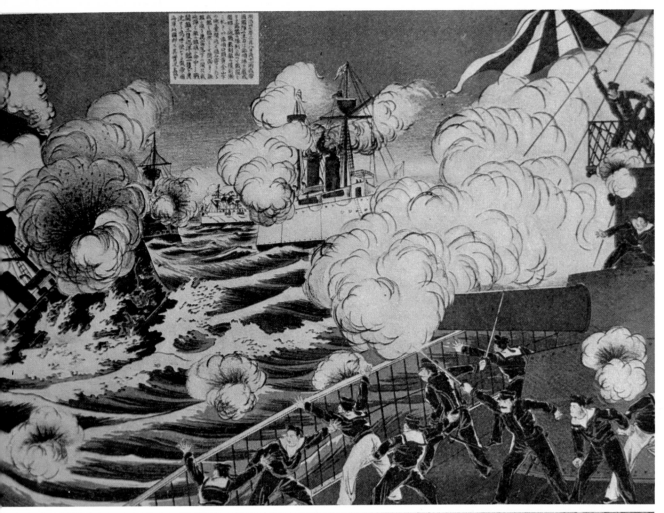

帝國艦隊旅順攻撃

115

Working Water

Rice

For three months of the year starting in late spring, sixty-five percent of the cultivated land is under water. Japan becomes a giant checkerboard of changing colors. On clear days bright blue squares of reflected sky; on dull days (and most days are at this time of the year), muddy brown or a cheerless gray that gives the water in the rice fields the illusion of great depth, though it is in fact but a few inches deep. Canals and water channels narrow as the water supply is stretched across the plains and tiny cascades tumble from level to level down the sides of the valleys. And in between are the sleepy expanses of the rice fields.

Soon the sleep is broken by farm women all tented up in their loose clothing with only their faces showing, and only their faces telling how many times before they have worked these fields. Walking backward, with backs bent, for days on end they plunge the rice shoots into the waiting mud. They leave behind them thin, straight lines of infant rice plants and equally straight lines of strange sunken footprints.

Most days it is raining and the sounds of rice planting are the sounds of water. Rain pelting on water, mud squelching, water splashing as bundles of young plants are thrown to the planters, and the swishing sounds of cords whipped across the water surface to help keep the lines straight.

It seems like only days after the planting is over that the spindly seedlings begin to thicken with lush green brushstrokes—from left to right, from north to south, this way, that way. Combinations of parallel curves and parallel straight lines produce strange perspectives. Hillsides become detailed contour maps. Now green stripes predominate, and the water is nearly hidden from view. A few more weeks and the fields will be thick with swaying leaves; the water that can no longer be seen will soon be totally consumed.

Fish

Fishing villages give off a clandestine air—a feeling of subterfuge, of activity hidden from all but the initiate. It is as though each is the headquarters of an underground resistance movement. The reason for this is simple. The timetable of a fishing village is unlike that of any other human settlement. Husbands leave their houses stealthily in the middle of the night and stride, hands thrust deep into their pockets and a look of grim purpose on their faces, toward the harbor. Without much noise they board their ships and depart. When the sun comes up, the village seems uninhabited. Smoke coils from chimneys but no people appear. Then suddenly there are children in the streets, chattering and playing, and it seems for a time like a village of orphans. It is not until the boats come in that the place behaves as one expects. But the period of visible activity is short. The fishermen go home to sleep, the women are shut in their fish factories preparing the fish for market, and the village is again deserted except for the children, who are now sitting about on the deserted boats, fishing and practicing to be fishermen. The tourists come by to experience life in a fishing village and can't find any.

The only time to see it all together is when the fish come in. That's when everyone is there and when for an hour or so the village is alive. The daily miracle of fish—hundreds, thousands, millions of fish. That the sea should offer up so many every day is beyond belief. Scientists point out that the well is not bottomless, but to the fisherman that is government talk. They're usually there, the fish, when he wants them, and if they're not it's because they're somewhere else. It couldn't be because there aren't any. In a country that has always lived from the sea, it is difficult to adjust to the possibility of its drying up.

After the fish are unloaded there are things for the men to do. Cleaning out the boat, stowing away the gear, checking the nets, a bit of maintenance on the engine. But it's all done quickly because sleep is tugging at them. It's mainly up to the women now. Standing ankle-deep in blood and guts they clean, salt, and pack the silver trophies for shipment to the market.

The pattern of life varies little from family to family or from generation to generation. Some get richer and build a new house higher up on the hill, but most stay as they are. And it's not necessarily a hard life. It's just a matter of what you're used to. Most of the young ones will follow in line, and their children too, so long as there are fish in the sea.

Seaweed

Seaweed is harvested in many parts of the world for the extraction of iodine or for use as a fertilizer, but in China and Japan it is mainly collected for food. For centuries Japanese women have dived for it or searched the shoreline for it, and they can still be seen around the coast, rummaging among the rocks like ragpickers.

Dozens of varieties of seaweeds are eaten in Japan: some are eaten fresh from the sea; others are used as flavoring in cooking; others are not eaten until they have been dried. As well as taking the natural harvest from the sea, the Japanese cultivate seaweed. *Nori* is the most commonly cultivated. Spores attach themselves to coarse nets that are stretched on bamboo poles across the surface of sheltered bays, and the seaweed grows on them. When the tide is high the nets are submerged. When the tide is low they hang in the air with festoons trailing down from the underside.

The seaweed is picked during the winter, dried, and pressed into thin, flat sheets brittle and shiny as black mica. These thin, tasty sheets become the indispensable wrapping for rice balls (*onigiri*) or for the many rice and fish delicacies of the *sushi* shop.

Pearls

Hanging in baskets tied to the rafts that float in Ago Bay a million million oysters are making pearls. To please the women of the world, these oysters have been plucked from the seabed and one by one subjected to surgery. A foreign body planted in the ovary causes them to secrete a pearly film that covers the irritant and makes its intrusion bearable. For three or four years they work at this, and what starts as a piece of shell the size of grape seed eventually becomes a pearl the size of a pea. For the duration of their contract the oysters are pampered. Food is plentiful, disease is guarded against, and in winter the rafts that hold them are towed hundreds of miles to the south where the water is warmer. At the end of their time, after all this care and attention, the oysters are slaughtered to retrieve the baubles they have created.

It was in the 1890s that Kōkichi Mikimoto founded Japan's cultured pearl industry. As a young man he became convinced that it was possible to stimulate the growth of a pearl in an oyster by implanting an irritant. When after many years of little or no success he finally found a suitable material to use as a nucleus, the poor Mikimoto soon became the very rich Mikimoto and an unknown name became world famous.

The *ama* spends her life diving to the bottom of the sea searching for oysters. She is better than a man at the job. She can stay underwater longer and she can stay in the water for a longer period. She is more productive. Young girls grow old in the sea and when the strain on their bodies becomes too much, they leave the sea and sit together on the shore making food and keeping a fire burning for their daughters.

Ama were diving for oysters long before the arrival of the cultured pearl. The search then was for natural pearls, and the harvest from Japan's seas was a rich one. Although it is now a major industry, the gathering of oysters is still an individual task. The boatmen keep an eye on them, but in effect the *ama* work alone, adrift in the sea, tied by fifty feet of rope to the floating tub in which they deposit their catch.

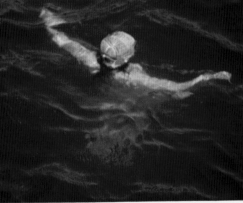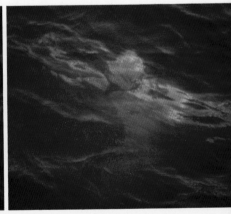

When they break the surface the *ama* make a whistling sound as the spent air is let slowly out of their lungs. This eerie whistle is called the "sound of the lonely beaches" (*isonageki*), and its haunting repetition comes across the water like the song of the sirens.

Timber

Water is put to work in many ways. Old
waterwheels are still turning in many places
in Japan and close by them giant hydroelectric
plants churn out enough power to light the
cities and run the factories that make steel
from iron ore and ships from steel. The waterways are still used as highways and down the
rivers and across the Inland Sea there is an
endless procession of barges and freighters.

The most colorful of the cargoes are the
logs of wood that are floated downstream and
then pulled in train to the timber districts. Up
to a hundred years ago it could be truly said
that Japan was made of wood. Its houses, tem-
ples and shrines, castles, bridges, and boats
were wood. More recently the cold grayness
of concrete has replaced many of the old wooden
structures, but there is still more wood to be
seen than in most parts of the world. Even
though the dense forests are kept renewed,
they can no longer supply all Japan's timber
needs. But the local supply is vast, and the job
of bringing it from the mountains to the saw-
mills in the cities is still the work of water.

The timber people are proud of their skills,
and there is no better occasion to see this than
at their annual festival. The loggers stage traditional displays of physical strength and balance,
making an entertainment out of the expertise
they use every day as they ride the logs or maneuver them into the tiny canals of the timber
district and deliver them to the doorsteps of the
timber merchants.

Cloth

Some rivers have been used for centuries, and still are, as part of the local craftsmen's plant. In Kyoto the Kamo River and the little streams that run off it are used to remove excess color from dyed and printed cloth. Lengths of cloth are thrown into the fast-flowing water, where they unfurl like battle banners and are left there bleeding until the dye has stopped coming out. Then they are plunged into boiling brine to fix the color and once again washed before being racked to dry in tall towers.

On Boys' Day in May proud families hang the traditional *koinobori* (streamers shaped like carp) from bamboo poles. In the little Shira-kawa river in Kyoto 30-yard lengths of newly printed cloth from which *koinobori* will be made are washed free of dye. It is fitting that fish which will spend their life in the sky should first be given a taste of river water. As the lengths of cloth curl back and forth the printed fish swim, as carp should, against the current. Later, filled with the wind, they will swim in the air in celebration of the future manly strength and tenacity of the male children of Japan.

Trade

It is curious that the Japanese have no history of seafaring. They were never masters of the sea like the Phoenicians or the Vikings or the Spanish or Portuguese. They have no great sailor like Ulysses, da Gama, Columbus, Magellan, or Cook. They did, of course, go to sea in wooden ships, and some of the more brazen adventurers engaged in piratical acts as far afield as the Philippines and Indochina. But even this was brought to a halt in the early part of the seventeenth century when Japan was closed to the world and the Japanese were prohibited from traveling abroad.

And yet Japan was designed to be a seafaring country. An extensive indented coastline with numerous sheltered harbors and the paucity of natural resources provided perfect conditions for its development as a maritime nation.

This natural destiny was quickly realized when the doors were opened in 1854. Fifty years later Japan had a merchant fleet of 1,500 vessels. A hundred years later it had wrapped the world in a spider's web of trade routes.

In all the major ports of the world you will find Japanese ships tied up. And Japanese ports seem like the busiest in the world. The busiest and the most crowded. Big ships sit in line waiting to be unloaded while all around them is a flurry of activity. Smaller boats—tugs, pilots, customs launches, police launches—hurry about their chores. The big ships are slow and cumbersome and the little ones buzz about them like parasite fish. The little ships are showoffs. They have the flair, they give the impression of daring. But the heroes are the big ships that have braved the dangers of the open ocean. It's the big sleepy ones that have seen the storms at sea and waves as high as mountains, winds or a cross swell that can shake loose a cargo and make it shift dangerously in the hold. It's the big ones that have plunged into a valley between waves and for the eternity of a few seconds have been totally submerged, only to rise again on the crest of the next wave and be left suspended in the air with propellers racing. The little ships rush about and puff and pant and impress us with their exertion. The big ones impress us with their dignity.

Water in Gardens

The ancient gardens of Egypt and Persia were geometric in design and contained within the courtyards of buildings. The ponds or reflecting pools so characteristic of these gardens were often simply storage tanks for the water that was in limited and sporadic supply. This formal courtyard garden, with water as a functional as well as decorative element, became and has remained the basic garden style throughout the Middle East and as far as India.

European gardens too have changed little down the years and though they are exterior gardens, they too are geometric in style. Harmony with the building seems to have been of greater importance than harmony with surrounding nature, and often they are little more than an extension of the work of the architect. Cascades, ponds, or fountains bear a strict geometric relationship to the buildings they adorn. In the eighteenth century several English gardeners rebelled against this architectural style and set out to copy nature. Soon the rich were converting their formal paths and flowerbeds into sweeping landscapes with artificial lakes and hills and "natural" forests and lawns. What we now know as the English garden is, like the Japanese, a "natural" garden, but its blowsy informality is in sharp contrast to the discipline of the Japanese garden.

The Japanese gardener learned his art from China, where a different sort of garden had developed quite independent of those in other parts of the world. The Chinese used the grandeur of nature as their model and created gardens on the same scale—great parks with lakes and islands and hills and waterfalls. The Japanese took the same elements and over the years modified the rules to suit the special conditions of their own land. Their gardens were smaller, effects more concentrated, nature more symbolically represented. The Japanese gardener

seems to have understood better than his teacher the intricacies of the relationships that exist among water, rocks, trees, and sky. He presents not the obvious or simple relationships but the more fundamental ones, the critical ones. Rocks tumble, mountains crack, water spills across barriers that fight to hold it back, trees lean perilously across streams or ponds in which reflections compete for one's trust.

Some aspects of Japanese gardens are felt rather than seen.

Lakes

In Japanese gardens water is used according to a number of traditional artistic or philosophical principles. Since the fundamental principle is to represent nature, even the smallest garden using water will present it in one of its natural forms—as a lake, a river, a waterfall.

Lakes came first in the history of Japanese gardens. Somewhere close to the year 600 a lake and island garden in the Chinese style was created for the empress Suiko, whose palace stood on the Nara plain. This was the first of the many lake gardens that were made thereafter. Some of these early artificial lakes still survive, although the oldest, that of the Shinsen-en in Kyoto, is now but a small pond, a remnant of the lake that existed there twelve hundred years ago.

In the lake or pond (*ike*), there is almost always an island, sometimes more than one, to reinforce the impression of a vast body of water. The islands are often symbolic. A turtle-shaped island, for example, is both a symbol of longevity and an allusion to the Taoist myth of the Isles of the Blest, islands inhabited by immortals and said to have floated in the sea on the backs of giant turtles.

The lake or pond is usually sited on the south side of a building, and the main rooms look out onto it. From inside one can see the reflection of bright blue skies, or waves breaking on the shore when the wind is strong, or raindrops creating a thousand steely circles. All the magic of the sea in all its moods is just a few feet away, and sometimes no more than a few feet across.

Rivers

Rivers (*yarimizu*) may be the only water in a
garden or they may play a secondary role
simply to feed and drain the pond. They too
have their traditional styles and symbolism.
Rivers symbolize the transience of life. They
must flow from east to west or from north to
south. The east is the source of purity, the
west is the outlet for impurities.

The *yarimizu* may flow swiftly and bubble
like a mountain stream, though more often it
winds slowly as a river does across a plain.
There will of course be obstructions to divert
its course—large boulders or an island to
divide it, or a fallen tree to make a dam. Its
course may be sandy or pebbly or rocky. And
there will be bridges of simple wooden planks
or massive slabs of stone.

Waterfalls

The garden manuals tell of a dozen or more different kinds of waterfall, but perhaps a sufficient classification is into three main types— cloth waterfalls (*nuno-ochi*), thread waterfalls (*ito-ochi*), and multistaged falls (*kasane-ochi*). The setting is as important as the fall itself. It is not a fountain and so it must fall naturally over a cliff, or through a crevice or down a tumble of rocks. Screened by trees to give it an added air of realism, the waterfall is often heard but not seen.

Even today, in the noise-polluted cities of Japan, one sometimes hears late at night the gentle splashing of a waterfall in someone's tiny suburban garden.

At the Water's Edge

At the water's edge
        there are mountains
        great granite shelves
                suspended
        there are mossy slopes
        and sparkling sunny places
        a coastline to be wondered at

At the water's edge
        there are beaches
                of crystal sand
                or glossy eggs of stone
        there are mud flats too
        and don't walk here signs
        mounds of flotsam leaves
                and little sticks
                stranded

At the water's edge
      there is a forest of cut-off trees
      stepping stones that march across the sea
      and sometimes there's a bridge
                a pier
                a pleasure boat
    or just a platform for the people of the sea
                to rest upon

Other Uses

Take a stone, hollow out a basin, pipe in a small flow of water and you have a *chōzubachi*. It's a drinking fountain, bird bath, reflecting pool, float bowl for fallen camellias or autumn leaves. It may be the only source of the sound of running water. In the past one was always located next to the toilet to wash the hands. Now its purpose is mainly decorative.

For gardeners troubled by deer or wild boar the answer is a deer-scarer (*shishi-odoshi*). This simple device is made from a piece of bamboo pivoted just off center so that it is slightly longer at the open end but slightly heavier at the closed end. If full of water it will tip up and spill out its contents; empty, it will fall back again. A supply of running water is all that is needed to maintain a perpetual motion. As the emptied bamboo pipe falls back again, it strikes a rock that has been strategically placed under it. The periodic clacking of bamboo on rock keeps the marauders away and adds another rhythmic sound to the garden.

Dry Water

The great raked sand garden of Ryōan-ji in Kyoto has been variously attributed, but there is little doubt that two men whose names are cut into the back of one of the fifteen stones used in the garden were very much involved in its construction. They may have been its designers as well. The names read Kotarō and Hikojirō, and it is known that they were two of the *kawaramono*.

The *kawaramono* (the riverbank people) were the lowliest of the lowly in the feudal structure. Apart from working at such tasks as butchering and tanning (which made them not only lowly but unclean), they were used as forced labor on public works. Hence their involvement in the building of gardens

It is thought that the *kawaramono* played a large part in the development of the *karesansui*, the raked sand gardens for which Japan is famous. Because they were unclean they were also unmentionable, and so there are no records to prove how significant their contribution really was. Whether they originated the idea or whether they simply executed the plans of some established garden designer is a debated point. It seems clear, however, that this kind of garden was perfected by the riverbank people.

In the latter half of the Muromachi period (1336–1568), the *karesansui* reached its most developed and most simple form. All but the most essential aspects of nature were one by one discarded until only two remained: rocks (the frame of nature symbolizing stillness) and sand (representing water and symbolizing movement and the transience of life). Out of these two elements great landscapes were created.

The same bare-bones principles apply to modern raked sand gardens, but even in the best examples, the heights reached by the *kawaramono* five hundred years ago have not been attained since.

How to Rake Water

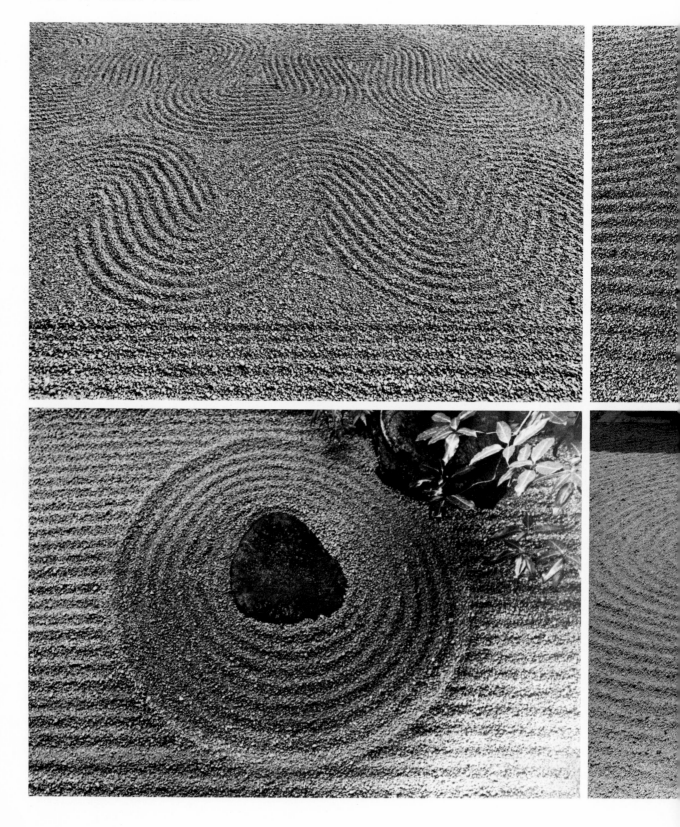

Water Gardens Now

As with most art forms, the day of private patronage has gone. New private gardens on the grand scale are rare, and most of the old ones have become public domain. Keeping alive the art of gardening has become the province of government and the larger commercial enterprises. One is more likely to find a masterpiece in a hotel or a factory than in a private house.

This is not surprising in view of the shortage of space and the astronomical costs involved. A single rock of moderate size may cost well over a thousand dollars. Enough to make a waterfall may cost a year's salary. Gardeners, like other artists, do not like to keep to budgets—particularly small ones—and there are few individuals who can contemplate incurring the costs of transplanting fully grown trees, of assembling fifty large rocks, and of providing a supply of several thousand gallons of water a day. Fortunately, the wealthier corporations have chosen to keep the art alive. It is rare for a multistoried building to be without its oasis of green trees and water splashing over rocks.

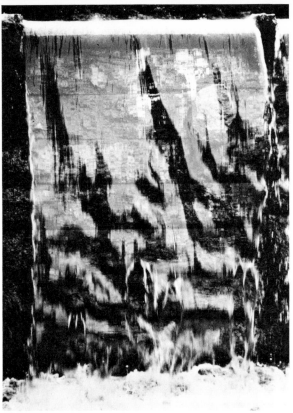

Water in Art

Japanese art was not "discovered" in Europe until the end of the last century. Van Gogh, Degas, Lautrec—in fact most of the painters of the period—knew it well and were to varying degrees influenced by it. A little later the Art Nouveau artists took it up with crusading fervor, and reputations like those of Beardsley, Mucha, Tiffany, Lalique, and a host of others were built on their facility, and in some cases their virtuosity, with what could be called "the Japanese line." A sinuous sweep that curls and ripples with a natural rhythm, there is no geometry about this liquid line. It is female mainly—a flamboyant gesture, yet the ultimate in mannerism.

In the seventh century Chinese painting styles were adopted by Japanese artists and for two centuries reigned supreme. During the Heian period the first indigenous style of major significance (*yamato-e*) emerged and with it came that great sweep of a line which was to remain from that point on one of the dominant elements in Japanese art.

Wherever there is water there is the line. Curving gently back and forth to indicate a lazy stream, eddying in circles when the stream flows faster as it might down a gentle hillside, springing up like a trampled thistle losing its seedpods when the water crashes against rocks, and humped in tall arches as ocean waves billow in the wind. The diversity of expression is remarkable, but an overriding similarity makes this manner of depicting water in art uniquely and perfectly Japanese.

For most Western painters water is color.

For most Japanese painters it is line.

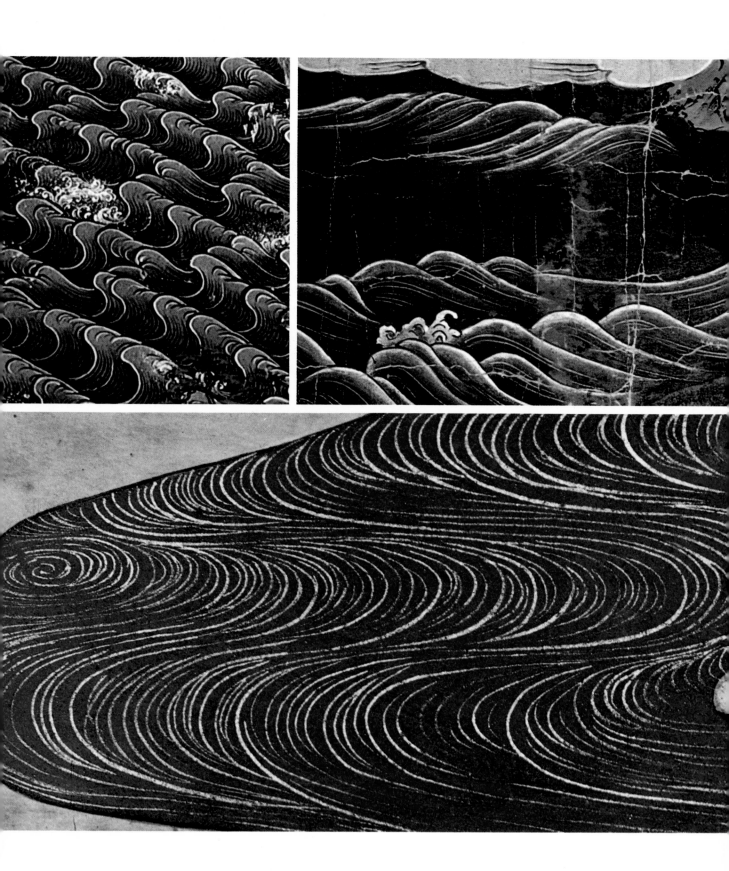

Hokusai

Hokusai, the woodblock printmaker of the eighteenth century, is unequaled as a master of water. No other artist before or since has given us a more comprehensive display of the many ways that water can be depicted. He was able with a minimum of fussiness to show water in all its moods. A few long, barely curving lines suggest the fastest-flowing current. A cluster of small dots becomes the frothing of water churned up by a dozen running feet. Near-semicircular curves suggest rolling waves that would rock a boat enough to make you seasick. Rapids are depicted by more irregular lines as the water bounces over rocks. A light breeze leaves ripples of unusual design on the surface. And, most famous of all, "the great wave" boldly holds itself aloft before crashing from the skies onto the boats that lie helpless beneath it.

Hokusai repeated his water patterns often, but so large was his repertoire that one can look at dozens of his woodblock prints and not find two in which he has drawn water in the same way.

Hiroshige

What Hokusai did with water his younger contemporary Hiroshige did with rain. The formula is a simple one—oblique parallel lines cutting across the foreground, a foreshortened perspective, the background in receding shades of gray like painted stage scenery. It is, however, the deviations from the formula or the incidental embellishments that give his rain pictures a realism which causes us mentally to turn up our collars as we look at them. Occasionally there are lines that cut across the parallels—rain falling in a different direction, suggesting a change of wind or giving the illusion of heavier rain. His people walk with hunched shoulders, leaning forward. Umbrellas seem difficult to hold and obviously inadequate. Birds fly home directly—in a straight line. Whatever he added to the basic formula, the end result was always a subtle expression of the smallness of man and the poetry of a rainy landscape.

Maki-e

In the dealer's shop there are pools of liquid gold. Fine threadlike currents flow round golden rocks and golden grasses bend toward the water's surface.

The shop has an ecclesiastical air. The attendants, like servants of God, unsmilingly and unflinchingly intone the exorbitant prices being asked for the objects that are to be sacrificed today. The prices seem so high for the objects are so small, but the beauty and intricacy of the work is ample justification.

The masters of *maki-e* (lacquer painting made with cut and powdered gold) for the most part work on small objects, such as little tea boxes. At first glance they are often deceptively simple, and the sheer difficulty of the work doesn't register until one looks very carefully.

The stylized water patterns, the exactly parallel lines, and the immaculate curves of waves and water are the most striking evidence of the extraordinary skill of the *maki-e* artist.

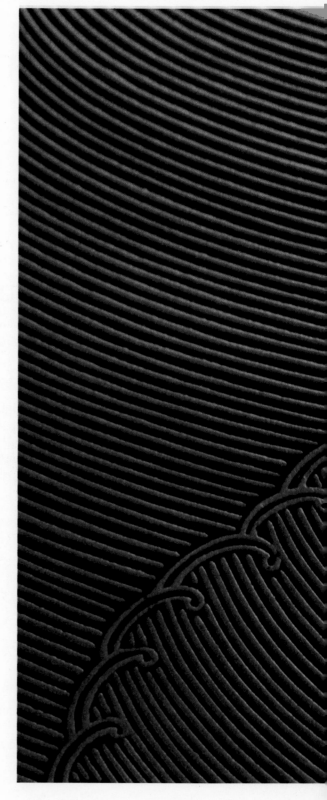

Ceramics

There is a dichotomy in Japanese ceramics: a style that stems directly from Chinese porcelains and a style native to Japan. The former is a highly decorated, delicate ware that never quite reached the heights of its Chinese forebears; the latter is more rugged, often undecorated, understated but with strong impact. In both these styles water patterns abound.

Among the porcelains a favorite theme is the rabbit romping through the ocean waves. To the Chinese and Japanese, the man in the moon is a rabbit, and the motif of a rabbit against a background of waves represents the moon reflected in the water.

Within the native Japanese pottery, water patterns are less formal, more impressionistic. But these simple, minimal designs are forceful and highly evocative. The simplicity of this native style is what attracted the Zen tea masters and it is primarily through tea-ceremony wares that Japanese pottery developed into the most expressive ceramic work the world has known.

The potter is at a considerable disadvantage to other artists in that he cannot see the result of his work until it has been processed by the fire of the kiln. Yet this must be for him a source of inspiration and excitement. There is part magic about the chemistry of glazes and the workings of the kiln; results are sometimes disappointing, sometimes far exceeding expectations. It seems ironical that rather nondescript gray and white painted designs can emerge from the holocaust of the kiln as glistening blue water.

Cloth, Wood, Paper, Metal

Friends of
Water

What do people get out of looking at water the way they do—gazing endlessly into its stillness or its changing patterns? What are they thinking of? Are they wondering where it came from or pondering its depth? Are they dreaming of infinity or looking for the life beyond it? Or is it just themselves that they are looking at, seeing more than they can see in a mirror?

People who have lived near the sea can seldom do without it. In the big cities one sees the students who've come from the sea towns sitting in parks staring into ponds. And salary-men retire and return to where they can hear the sound of water or see the sun falling behind the waves.

Most city people are satisfied with smaller doses and in the season take a picnic by the sea. Like going to the zoo. But all the animals of the zoo are equal to only one small expanse of water, which is enough to hold one's attention a whole day through.

The Old Man Who Knows About the Sea

The old man who knows about the sea. And about boats. Lonely now because his mates have almost all gone, all but a few who are too old or too sick to remember. But he remembers well, and every day walks down to the sea, only a few steps really, to check things. The weather, the condition of the boats, the size of the catch, the prices the robbers are offering for the fish, and the tall stories that are not much taller really than they were in his day. He checks silently. For he is not a part of it any more. Although they let him have a place at the table, they don't deal him any cards. And yet he knows it all. He could tell them if they'd let him. He understands the sea and loves it for the good and the bad of it. But when he tries to tell them how to beach a boat when the sea is choppy and they are having trouble, they don't hear his voice. They don't see that he is speaking.

Sometimes he talks to the sea instead.

Fishing

Fishing is
a sport
or an outdoor activity
or a pastime
or a game
or a hobby
or an art
or whatever it is
that fishing is.

Boats on the Water

It is interesting how a character can change the moment a person steps onto a boat. Someone who will usually avoid looking at strangers, out of modesty or politeness, will, the moment a boat has pulled away from the shore, wave enthusiastically to any passing human being. On the water everyone is a friend.

Very few are dwarfed by a boat however big it may be. Usually the reverse happens: people become larger than life. In rowboats the rower becomes a minor Hercules pulling the world beneath him with his oars and the lady being rowed becomes a runaway princess enchanted by her new freedom and, of course, by her oarsman.

And boat captains are a very special breed. They have eyes which see great distances and they can feel the tides and smell the weather. They are kings of tiny states, but at most times they barely notice their subjects. Their minds are always on the sea.

Boats are teamwork.

Boats are total isolation.

An Outing on the River

At the Hozu Bridge a dozen or more boats maneuver into position and approach the loading ramp one at a time. Having registered their names and paid for their tickets, people wait to be called over the loudspeakers, which tell them that they can now enter Boat 73 along with fifteen or so other passengers who will take the exciting ride downstream. For the next two hours the boatmen (three to a boat) will push, row, and guide the adventurers in among craggy boulders, through shallows that seem no more than ankle-deep, between the perpendicular walls of narrow gorges, and downhill over the noisy white water of the rapids.

The course is not a hair-raising experience. The excitement we all feel is due to the oddity of what we are doing rather than to the risks we are taking. The flat-bottomed boat sometimes scrapes itself across the rocky shallows, sometimes strikes a submerged boulder, or passes a cliff face with less than an inch to spare. But it is a sturdy boat and the boatmen know their way around. The squeals of excitement and the mock cries of fright are the acting out of an imagined recklessness far removed from reality. In fact, it is a rather peaceful two hours. Apart from the occasional squeals, it is very quiet on the river and one can hear the constantly changing sounds of the water. Through the shallows the sound is like the chattering of a flock of very small birds—animated, vapid, full of sparkle. In the calm pools the water is deeper and the sound is silence, an eerie nothingness except for the plop of an oar. It is here that the resonant thump of a sub-merged rock sounds so scary and the overreaction of the passengers splits the silence. In the steeper rapids the water is noisy, splashing over the rocks and greeting the boat with a hearty smack on the bows. Sometimes it turns round and comes back at the boat, breaking like surf as we push through it.

Along the banks watching our silent or noisy progress moves a procession of picnickers—families with young children carrying butterfly nets, students carrying guitars, old men with fishing rods; everyone carrying lunch boxes, packets of dried squid, Coca-Cola in cans, and sakè in gigantic bottles. This is the cherry blossom season. Picnicking under the blooming trees is an old tradition, and for the men particularly, finishing the cherry blossom picnic somewhere between slightly tipsy and excessively drunk is very much a part of that tradition. The Hozu River is lined with cherry trees and the picnickers scatter themselves over the rocky banks. Everybody is taking pictures of us, of themselves, of the cherry blossoms and the red camellias that are falling from trees fifty feet high and floating downstream. Everybody is enjoying the river.

A final turn and we have reached the end of the rapids and the end of our excursion. Ahead is the ancient Togetsu Bridge at Arashiyama. Our boat will be loaded onto a truck and taken back to the Hozu Bridge, where another group is waiting to board No. 73 and ride the rapids.

Paddling and Swimming

There's an element of daring in paddling in the sea or sitting with one's feet in it. It's a sort of flirtation. Children shriek with excitement as the waves break round their ankles enticing them to go a little farther. And the old remember the games of youth that are now beyond them and explore the possibilities of satisfaction from the games of children.

Swimming is a more full-blooded affair, but Japan is a nation of bathers rather than swimmers. Most Japanese "swim" in the bath long before they step into the sea. And most of the millions who flock to the beaches and the swimming pools in the summer are really taking a bath. They like to keep their feet firmly on the bottom and much of the bobbing and floating and splashing is bath behavior. Only a few are true swimmers. These are the ones who find water a challenge and must fight it until they are defeated. And yet exhausted by it, conquered by it, they take up the challenge again and again and go back for more. Swimming is a lusty pastime.

Ame Ame Fure Fure

The English children's song says "Rain, rain, go away"; the Japanese children's song says "Rain, rain, please come."

Miscellaneous Friends

The *mizusumashi* walks on water and doesn't get his feet wet. He darts and dashes across a pond or a calm patch of river or lake in the hunt for food. Although he can't eat very much by the looks of things—he's so skinny that surface tension makes solid enough ground for him to land on.

The tortoise needs a rock or a lily pad to hold him up. Head in the air and the rest underwater is his preferred position. Cool and curious—that's the tortoise.

Is it greed or love that keeps seabirds so close to the water, even after they've had their fill? Sometimes it seems as though they're tied to it by strings like so many remote-controlled models swooping and wheeling, wheeling and swooping in a never-ending loveplay with the waves. There's so much sky above but they use so little of it, as if they might miss something if they soar too high. And when they're not in the air you find them hopping along the waterline just where the waves slip back across the sand or sitting in rows on rocks with necks stretched up like a choir serenading the sea.

Wherever there is life-supporting water there is a population of living creatures—insects, fish, birds, mammals—living in or off it. Sometimes their presence goes unnoticed, for many are creatures of camouflage and concealment. Crabs and shellfish bury themselves under the sand and rising bubbles are the only clue to their existence. Smaller creatures remain forever invisible to the naked eye. A distant fountain in the sea may be all that one sees of a giant whale.

If one stands for long enough on the shore, in the shallows where animal life began, one can still observe the links in the chain of development from fish to amphibian that led eventually to man. And here one can see the constantly changing balance of life that in the future will cause further development or perhaps extinction. Man is having greater and greater influence for better or worse on the state of this balance, and the fate of waterbugs and whales depends on his good sense and sensibilities.

Carp in the Sumida

As we traveled around Japan we saw and photographed water which was beautiful, exciting, mysterious. We also saw a lot of water which was disgustingly polluted and we often wondered if a point of no return had not already been passed. But here and there we saw efforts being made and evidence that the long journey back has been started. The newspapers are full of it. Government spokesmen talk of how much is being done and old men write letters saying they've seen fish in places where there haven't been any fish for years. Carp are once again living in Tokyo's Sumida, a river that has long been little better than a cesspool.

It will be a long time before all the dead waters are teeming with life again, but the survival of carp in the Sumida is a good omen.

NOTES ON THE PHOTOGRAPHS

HOKKAIDO

● SAPPORO

1
2

N SEA

4   3

5

6

7

HONSHU

13

14

OTO 19
20 ●
● 21
OSAKA

12   TOKYO
● 8

15   10
11

16

18 17

9

PACIFIC   OCEAN

ACKNOWLEDGMENTS

Our thanks to Fred Harris, Emily Seaman, Masajiro Shimamura, Akiko Koike, and Mary and Jerry Swartz for their help during the preparation of this book, and especially to Sachiko Suzuki for her generous contributions.

Without the careful planning of Saeko Sato and Masanori Eto, our many trips to distant parts of Japan would have been far more difficult and far less productive.

To Jeannine Ciliotta, the editor of this book, our gratitude for her tireless assistance when it was most needed.

B.B.
D.L.

PHOTOGRAPHER'S NOTE

The photographs in this book were shot primarily with Nikon equipment. I used a nine-year-old Nikon F, a Nikon Photomic FTN and a Nikomat EL for 90 percent of the pictures and a 6×7 Asahi Pentax for the remainder. A good percentage of the Nikon pictures were shot with the 55mm Micro-Nikkor, an incredibly sharp and versatile lens that allows one to focus from about 6 inches to infinity. Other lenses used were 24mm, 50mm, 105mm, 200mm, and 500mm Nikkors. When I had to carry all my own gear or wanted to travel light, I used two Nikon bodies and just two lenses, usually the Micro and the 200.

The 35mm color photographs were shot on Kodachrome–X, Kodachrome II, Ektachrome–X, or when light was insufficient, high-speed Ektachrome. 120 Ektachrome–X was used in the Pentax.

Most of the black and white pictures were shot on Tri–X and developed in Microdol. Occasionally where very limited light was available Tri–X was pushed from its normal ASA 400 to 1200 by developing in Acufine. Some Fuji SS film was also used.

A photographer needs good equipment; he also needs the right kinds of experience and guidance. For being fortunate enough to have had that experience and that guidance, I owe Don Nichols, teacher and friend, a very special thanks.

The "weathermark" identifies this book as a publication of John Weatherhill, Inc., publishers of fine books on Asia and the Pacific. Editor in charge, Jeannine Ciliotta. Book design, layout, and typography, Dana Levy. Production supervision, Mitsuo Okado. Composition, General Printing Company, Yokohama. Printing, Nissha Printing Company, Kyoto. Binding, Okamoto Binding Company, Tokyo. The type of the main text is set in 12-pt Monotype Bell with hand-set Bell and photo-set Palatino for display.